Muriel McDonald, Gilmour McDonald,
Marjorie McDonald, and Erling McDonald

Muriel Remembers

by
Muriel McDonald

ASPECT Books
www.ASPECTBooks.com

Copyright © 2011 Muriel McDonald
ISBN-13: 978-1-57258-648-2 (Paperback)
ISBN-13: 978-1-57258-845-5 (ePub)
ISBN-13: 978-1-57258-952-3 (Kindle/Mobi)
Library of Congress Control Number: 2011902723

Published by
ASPECT Books
www.ASPECTBooks.com

Contents

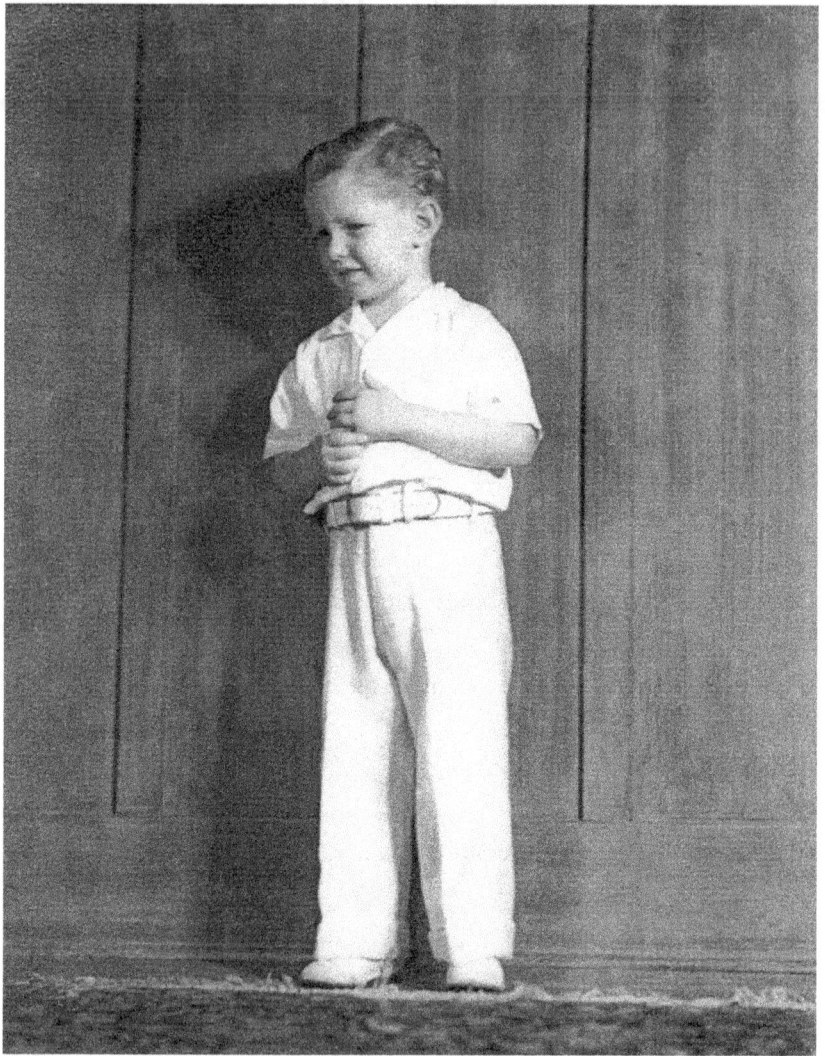

Erling

Chapter 1

My Brother

Have you ever thought about how wonderful it is to have a brother or sister? I am so lucky to have had the privilege of having a brother ever since 1939, the year I was born.

Erling, my brother, is someone you can always count on through thick and thin, no matter what. He is five years older than I am, which was such a big help while I was growing up. He was much more knowledgeable than I, in addition to being physically bigger, which was a blessing too.

Erling has dark brown (almost black) kind eyes and beautiful golden brown wavy hair. When he smiles at you it makes you feel special, like you are someone important.

During World War II, we walked everywhere, even to church. Dad used to offer his arm to mom whenever we were dressed up to go somewhere special. When Erling saw Dad do this, he would offer me his arm. That always made me feel so important and grown up.

Erling's friends always accepted me and told me I was their friend. Many of them sang in the Takoma Boy's Choir that my dad directed. I felt so respected even though I was little.

I started school when I was seven years old. Erling had a bicycle, and I would sit on the bar in front of him and hold our lunch bags as he pedaled to school. After riding down a big hill, which was quite exciting, we would arrive at Sligo School.

As I started school, Erling gave me some advice and told me that if anyone tried to bully me I was to tell them that I had a big brother. Not long afterwards, David Dilldine, one of my classmates, said to me, "I'm going to beat you up."

He was actually a cute little boy who was trying to be tuff, but I wasn't going to put up with his meanness, so I said, "You better not, I have a big brother!"

David quickly responded, "I have a big brother, too, and he will beat your brother up."

I looked at him and said, "He better not, my brother is much bigger than your brother."

David decided to drop it. He crossed the street and left me alone. Can you see how important a brother is? David never gave me any more trouble.

When I saw Erling later that day, I told him what happened. He just smiled and that was all there was to that.

In the winter, Erling used to take me sledding. We only had one sled, so I would lie down on his back and hug him around the neck as we sped down the hill. It was fun, and Erling was a safe driver. It was really a long walk to the top of the hill for my little legs, so Erling would say, "You sit on the sled, and I'll pull you." Then when he got tired, he would ask me to walk. Erling always tried to look out for me. He was so kind and such a gentleman, always thinking of ways he could help.

On the other hand, sometimes we could be live wires, as Dad used to say. I remember one time after Erling had heard a story about a flying carpet. Erling and I often took things literally, which made for hysterical experiences. He decided to show me what a flying carpet was, so he took a little oriental rug in the upstairs hall, sat me down in front of him, pulled the rug up in front of us, and sent us sailing—bumpity, bump, bump—down the stairs. Since that was rather uncomfortable, we decided to discontinue that idea.

While I was growing up, Erling built a tree house. Actually, it was several boards nailed together to form a platform, but we called it a tree house. Because I was too little to climb the tree, Erling nailed small pieces of wood on the tree trunk to make steps for me. To celebrate the completion of our tree house, my mom made egg salad sandwiches. Erling helped me climb the tree, then he went and got our special lunch. Those sandwiches were especially delicious because we ate them in our tree house.

Another one of my fondest memories is when I attended symphony concerts with Erling. He loved the music as much as I did, so we always had a wonderful time. He would hand me his binoculars, and then he would poke me in the ribs and softly sing a note. His little game required me to figure out what instrument was playing the note. If I made a mistake, he would help me, and then he would grin from ear to ear.

Erling was a wonderful big brother. He was always interested in what I was doing. Erling used to ask me to sit on the basement steps and read to him while he worked on piano actions. He knew it would help me to read better if I practiced though he never mentioned this as it might have hurt my feelings. Whatever was important to me was important to Erling, like playing or singing in a recital or at church. He was always encouraging. This meant the whole world to me as his little sister.

Erling grew to be a fine gentleman. At 6 foot 2 inches tall, he was handsomely built with chiseled features like our dad. His heart is so big that it seems almost like he knew Jesus like the disciples. His everyday language is interspersed with truths from the Bible and Ellen G. White's writings.

I am so fortunate to have a brother like Erling Spencer McDonald. He is a blessing to those around him, especially to me!

Chapter 2

The Indian Feast

While I was growing up, my Aunt Lorraine loved to entertain, and she did this often. Sometimes she asked my mother and me to help prepare the food, which was quite a lot of fun. For instance, we made fancy sandwiches, which were lots of work but were very delicious, for her parties.

One time Aunt Lorraine invited the Votaws, missionaries from India, to make an Indian dinner for her family, my family, grandma and grandpa, and their own family. This was quite an undertaking, and it took many hours to prepare.

The Votaws had been missionaries in India for so many years that it seemed like they were Indians themselves. They loved the people and the culture of India.

The Votaws told Aunt Lorraine what spices and ingredients to buy so that the Indian recipes would be authentic. The food they prepared was a typical Indian meal that consisted of many courses. It turned out to be a feast.

There were approximately twenty people to feed, which was quite a lot of people. They started cooking in the morning to be ready to start serving dinner in the late afternoon.

I remember the delicious food. One of my favorite dishes was an amazing dessert made with coconut milk. The batter was then poured into a coconut shell with a hole drilled in the bottom. The batter dripped through the hole into hot oil to fry. The long pieces of this delicate concoction was then dipped into honey. It was delicious to say the least.

A little while before dinner was ready, Mrs. Votaw told us kids that she had something special for us. She had brought saris for the girls to wear and the typical men's national costume for the boys. She knew exactly how to fold a sari and put it on. It was almost unbelievable. To make a sari, she took a straight piece of cloth, folded it and made pleats for the skirt in front, and then tucked it in at the waist. Then she draped it over our shoulder or on our heads. It is extremely clever. We were very pleased with these native costumes from India. What fun! It was almost like we were in India.

Next, she gave us a lesson in the customs of India. For instance, you must sit on the floor when you eat dinner. And you must always eat with your right hand. You put your fingers together to form a cup, and then you pick up your food. They do not use silverware. Meals are served one course at a time with only one food on your plate at a time. We were served rice and curry for one course, and rice and dhal for one course, etc., all of which was quite delicious. I wish I could remember all the courses we had in detail. However, I do remember that they were all very good. And, of course, the food tasted better because I was wearing a sari, sitting on the floor, eating with my fingers, and pretending I was in India.

India is a fascinating country with a very interesting culture. If I had a chance to eat a dinner like the wonderful Indian meal I enjoyed at Aunt Lorraine's house many years ago, I'd jump at the chance.

Chapter 3

My Little Friend

When I was a little girl, I was very fortunate to have a best friend. She was my next door neighbor. We had a special bond. She was slight in build, with blue eyes and blond hair.

We did everything together and were quite inseparable. One day my little friend came to me and said, "You are really lucky, because you have a grandmother."

I looked at her, surprised at what she was saying. I said, "You don't?"

With a sad expression on her face, she simply said, "No."

I was caught off guard and saddened at my friend's response. "What happened?" I asked. She then told me the story, "Well, you see, my mommy and daddy were both orphans."

I was startled at this revelation. "I didn't know that!"

She continued, "Well, they were. My dad's mommy and daddy died and my mom's mommy and daddy died when they were little, and they both grew up in orphanages. That is where my parents met."

I looked at her serious little face with great big sad eyes. I felt terrible about her loss, so I tried to comfort her.

Finally, she looked at me and shyly asked, "Do you think that your grandma would be willing to be my grandma too?"

Surprised, I said, "I don't know. You would have to ask her. Let's go and ask my mommy what she thinks."

My little friend nodded and said, "Would you please ask your mommy for me?"

I told her I surely would, so off we went to find my mom. When we found her, I said, "My friend doesn't have any grandparents. Her mommy and daddy grew up in orphanages because their parents died when they were little. Isn't that terrible?"

My mommy looked at us and agreed that it was very sad that my little friend didn't have any grandparents. Then I told my mommy of my little friend's wish that my grandma could be her grandma too. I said, "Do you think Grandma White would be willing to be my little friend's grandma?"

Mom smiled at us with a twinkle in her eye. She said, "You know, I can't answer for grandma. I have just a little more work to do here and then, if you would like, I will take you to grandma's house in the car, and you can ask her if she would be willing to be a grandma to your little friend."

Just a few minutes later, Mom said she was ready to take us to grandma's house. You could tell that she thought that what we were thinking was really important.

When we got to Grandma White's house, my little friend whispered to me, "Would you mind asking your grandma if she would be my grandma for me? I'm afraid to ask."

I assured her that if she was bashful I would do the talking. But mom brought it up first. She said to grandma, "These little girls have an important question to ask you."

My little friend shrank behind me, hiding. I got all my courage up and took my little friend's hand and brought her forward, "Grandma, did you know that my little friend doesn't have a grandma. Her grandparents died long before she was born. They died when her mommy and daddy were little kids, which is why her parents grew up in an orphanage."

Grandma looked sympathetically at the two of us. She said she was terribly sorry about my friend's loss.

Encouraged by her sympathetic response, I went on, "Grandma, my little friend wants to know if you think you could be her grandma, too, because she doesn't have a grandma of her own. Would you be her grandma, please?"

My grandma smiled all over. Then she said, "I would love to be your grandma. And you know, I will ask my husband if he will be your grandpa. But I am sure he will say that he wants to be your grandpa too. And would you please tell your big brother and big sister that we would love to be their grandma and grandpa too."

My dear little friend quickly forgot her bashfulness. She said that she would remember to tell her brother and sister that Grandma White said that she and her husband wanted to be their grandparents. Before we left, Grandma White made it official by reminding my friend to call her grandma. "Please call us grandma and grandpa from now on, and tell your brother and sister to do the same."

Chapter 4

Great Grandma's Mittens

The snow was beautiful and lots of fun. It was noon, and I had just come in from playing outside all morning. I was cold through and through. I took off my coat, cap, mittens, socks, and boots. I put my mittens and socks on the big old radiator to dry. After laying my things out to dry, I rested both of my hands on the radiator to warm them up. It felt so good! As soon as they warmed up, I lay on the floor and put my feet on the radiator. My feet were so cold that they felt stiff, but it wasn't long until the radiator had warmed up my toes so that I felt much better.

I was starving after that much exercise, so I went into

the kitchen to see what mom had made for lunch. She usually made homemade potato soup (which I loved) or Campbell's thick black bean soup (which I also loved) when it snowed heavily. This particular day she had made egg salad sandwiches to go with the potato soup with celery and carrots sticks on the side. She knew we (me, my brother and dad) would all be extra hungry.

After lunch was over and mom and I did the dishes and cleaned up the kitchen, I went to check on my mittens and socks to see if they were dry. Wouldn't you know, they were all still wet. I went upstairs and got a clean dry pair of socks to wear. That wasn't a problem. But the mittens were another matter. I did not have another pair. I went to my mother and told her of my dilemma. "Come with me," she said, so I followed her to her room.

She opened her cedar chest that Dad had made for her. (Dad had made forty cedar chests by hand to pay for his entrance fee to college. He had sold all except three, one of which he saved for his future wife.) After looking under some things, mom stood up with something black in her hands.

"Do you promise to be very careful with these mittens if I let you wear them?" Mom said. "My Grandma Eastman, your great grandma, knitted them for me when she was blind."

I promised my mom that I would be very careful with the treasured mittens. Mom said that Great Grandma Eastman lived to be ninety years old and that she became blind the very last part of her life. Great Grandma Eastman liked to be busy, so even after she became blind, she kept her hands busy by knitting. She could tell if she had dropped a stitch through her sense of touch, and she would ask my mother to be her eyes for her and pick up the stitch she had dropped. After Great Grandma Eastman finished knitting these wool mittens, she used a special technique of using warm water and rubbing the mittens between her hands to make them wind resistant and water repellant.

I wore those mittens all afternoon. They were the warmest mittens I had ever worn. When I came back from playing, mom helped us make maple syrup with sugar, water, and maple flavoring. We boiled the syrup, and then poured the boiled syrup on the snow outside. This process is called "sugaring off," and it makes a delicious maple candy. We all loved it! Even Cooky my dog loved "sugaring off," but the most fun was laughing at her as she tried to chew the sticky candy, which made her jaws look like they were stuck together.

I was very careful to give the precious mittens back

to my mom at the end of the day. They were a piece of our family history, a reminder of my Great Grandma and Great Grandpa Eastman who lived on a farm in Minnesota. They raised everything, including sheep that provided wool for Great Grandma Eastman. She carded, spun, and knitted mittens, socks, and hoods for her family from the wool their sheep produced.

I cherish the stories of my family and the people they loved.

Chapter 5

Punch and Judy

When I was young, my brother, Erling, loved nature. Mom and Dad encouraged this interest, especially since Ellen G. White recommends the study of nature.

Erling was so interested in nature that he was made an honorary member of the Biology Club of Washington Missionary College, which was close to our home. The biology professor and the club members loved him and all the interesting animals and plants he collected for them to study and appreciate. He was so inquisitive that he would ask questions that would even make the biology professor think.

When Erling was in the fifth grade, if I remember correctly, and about 11 years old, he read an ad in *Popular Me-*

chanics that talked about buying raccoons from a fur farm. He wrote to the fur farm and asked them questions about the raccoons. He found out that he could buy a female raccoon that had been bred for $50.

Well, Erling did not have $50, but he was extremely industrious and quite capable. He got busy and went to work mowing lawns for our neighbors. He worked and worked, earning a few cents for each lawn mowing job he did. He was persistent, and he slowly raised the money by doing odd jobs and mowing lawns.

I do not remember exactly how long it took, but I think it was quite a few months. He worked all summer and into the winter, switching to shoveling snow instead of mowing lawns.

In school, Erling was taking a carpentry class, which he thoroughly enjoyed. Erling was really good at working with his hands, so he designed and built a house for his future raccoons. He chose a hard wood. And Dad gave him shingles just like the ones on our house to put on his little house. The house had an unusual door with nice brass hinges on the side and near the top so that the door could open from the side or swing open and closed.

If Erling did not want the door to swing open, he could latch it closed. That way he could keep the raccoons in their house if necessary. The floor of the house had a golden yellow linoleum floor made from a piece of linoleum left over from when Dad remodeled our kitchen.

Erling put wheels on the house so that it could be moved, allowing him to clean under it. He was close to being done, when the female raccoon arrived. She came in a heavily built strong wooden box. She was very ferocious. There were strong wires on one end of the box to allow her fresh air and a view. Erling begged Dad and Mom to let him put the mother raccoon in our basement, which had a cement floor, until he finished the pen for the raccoon. Mom and Dad agreed to his plan.

Erling coaxed and coaxed the mother raccoon with sugar lumps. If he talked softly to her, she would look at him and be quiet, but she would not come and take the sugar lumps from his hand. Sometimes he would drop the sugar lumps on the floor, and she would grab it with her dexterous paws, which looked like little hands. She would look the sugar over, turning it over and over before taking a small bite. You could see then she was pleased as she ate the sugar. Then Erling would coax her again, placing the sugar closer to him so she would learn not to be afraid. He did this quite a few times. Then he said to me, "Muriel, see if she will come to you and take the sugar from your hand.

You must be very careful and hold your hand completely flat so that she will not bite you." He demonstrated how I should hold my hand. Then Erling said, "I don't think she is as afraid of you because you are littler."

I grinned all over. I agreed to help try to tame the mother raccoon and see if she would take sugar from my hand. I softly talked to her and asked if she would like a sugar lump. She looked at me curiously and came toward me a little bit. Then she stopped and looked at me again. So I coaxed her and offered the sugar again. She was quite nervous, but she ran and grabbed the sugar cube from my hand. Then she ran under the laundry tubs and ate it. We were both extremely pleased.

Erling soon finished the pen and put the house in it. And then he put the mother raccoon in the house. She acted pleased with all the space in the pen and the nice house. The mother raccoon became tame enough to take lumps of sugar from Erling's hand, but that was all. Erling became worried because she had not had her babies, so he called the zoo. The zookeeper told him not to bother her because if she was afraid she might eat her babies. He told Erling not to give her any sugar now. He told him to leave her alone. Erling was really frightened. He was so scared that he did not even go in to the pen.

Late one Friday afternoon after I was all ready for Sabbath, I went and sat quietly next to the raccoon pen. A few minutes later I heard this trilling noise. I was really excited, but I knew I must be extremely quiet, so I tiptoed into the house and ran and told Erling that I thought the baby raccoons had been born. Naturally, Erling immediately went out to the pen to quietly check on the situation. Sure enough, the baby raccoons had been born. He gave the mother some sugar and left her alone like he had been told.

Well, you wouldn't believe what happened next. The mother raccoon and all four babies escaped out of the pen. Erling was heartbroken. The tears ran down his cheeks, and he sobbed and sobbed. I cried too. In fact, our whole family was really upset. We all knelt down and prayed earnestly that we could find our little raccoon family and put them back in their home.

Erling called the veterinarian. The vet said, "I do not know anything about raccoons. You can get a coon hound, but the coon hound will catch the raccoon mother and her babies and kill them." That's all the veterinarian knew.

Well, Erling did not think that was a good plan, so he called the zoo, and once again, the zookeeper talked to Erling and gave him advice. In fact, he said, "Try to find the raccoons, and then call me back. We have a big butterfly net made of strong rope, and we will come and help you catch her when you find her."

I listened as Erling talked on the telephone. Then I decided to start looking for the raccoons. I prayed silently to God to help me find Erling's pets. I even prayed silently during my search. I looked in the alley behind the garage, and there I heard the baby raccoons trilling. I followed the sound until I saw two eyes that looked like lights—I thought they were the eyes of one of the babies. I tiptoed back to the house to find Erling. When I told him I found the raccoons, he came quietly with me to double check. We did not make a peep. Then we went back to call the zookeeper for help.

There were about five men who came out immediately from the zoo with a huge butterfly net made of ropes. They asked Erling where the raccoons were. He quietly showed them. Everyone was really quiet until they were in position to catch the mother raccoon.

The men were really nice, although they looked pretty tough. They knew what they were doing, and they were kind. They scared the mother, and she ran, leaving her babies. The men ran after her until they caught her. One of the men retrieved the four babies, which he could hold in his large hand. The babies looked like little gray mice with rings on their tails. Their eyes were still closed, and they did not have masks on their little faces yet. The baby raccoons were awfully cute, to say the least! We thanked the zookeeper.

Before the men left, the zookeeper told Erling to install turkey wire on the sides of the pen. He told us that raccoons can pull chicken wire apart, so we needed the heavier wire The zookeeper put the mother raccoon and babies in the little house and closed the door so they could not get out until the turkey wire was up.

Erling tried and tried to tame the mother raccoon, but she was just too wild. She had never been handled by a human being when she was small, so it was too late to really make her a friendly pet. The mother raccoon escaped from her pen two more times, and Erling had to install a cement floor so that she could not dig out. She was quite intelligent and very capable.

One day Erling was feeding her sugar lumps when one of her babies walked up to get a lump of sugar from Erling. The mother raccoon bit the baby, picked it up, and put it in a corner of the little house. The mother raccoon was a good disciplinarian, but she was not tame. This really upset Erling, so he talked to the zookeeper—they had become good friends. The zookeeper told Erling that he must take the babies away from the mother raccoon or he would not be able to tame the babies because she was so wild and ferocious.

Kittens and puppies can drink milk out of a saucer when they are six weeks old, so when the baby raccoons were six weeks old, we thought they would be able to drink milk out of a saucer. But baby raccoons drink like a horse, and they cannot drink milk out of a saucer by themselves when they are six weeks old.

The zookeeper had told Erling that the zoo would take the mother and keep her, and if ever he wanted her back, the zoo would give her back to him. Erling had already taken the mother raccoon to the zoo, so now he had to figure out how to feed the babies when they could not drink out of a saucer.

Erling asked me for a doll bottle. The nipple was too stiff. He tried a baby bottle, but the nipple was too big—it would not even go into the little raccoons tiny mouths. What was Erling going to do?

Aunt Winnie—Winnifred McCormack—rented a room in the upstairs of our house. Although she wasn't our real aunt, she was very special to our family, and we adopted her as our own. She was head of nursing education for the General Conference of Seventh-day Adventists, traveling all over the world to help with nursing education.

At this time, Aunt Winnie was home, so Erling told her about his problem of feeding the baby raccoons. She told him to go to The Washington Sanitarium and Hospital and tell the nurses in the nursery about his tiny raccoons. Aunt Winnie said, "Ask the nurses in the nursery if they have a premature nursing bottle." Aunt Winnie knew just what kind of bottle to ask for because she had special training in the care of newborns. Erling immediately went to The Washington Sanitarium and Hospital and got special permission to talk to the nurses in the nursery. (At that time, you had to be sixteen to visit the nursery and look in the window at the babies. This was to protect them from infection and give the new mothers a chance to rest and get their strength back before they went home.)

The nurses were very sympathetic and said that, yes, they would give him a premature nursing bottle for his baby raccoons. This was really wonderful. The bottle had an extremely soft nipple that was very little. On the end of the bottle was a syringe so that you could force feed the babies if they were too weak to suck.

Well, you know what, the premature nursing bottle was just perfect. The little raccoons would wrap all four paws around the bottle while they drank. They were absolutely precious. Raccoons are from the bear family, and they looked like little teddy bears with masks on their faces.

Erling and I fed the little raccoons a mixture of half canned milk and half water, just like you would a kitten.

But something terrible happened! All the babies got diarrhea and became terribly sick, so sick that they could not eat. Erling and I prayed again that Jesus would heal the adorable precious pet raccoons. I really believe God answered our prayers. It says in the Bible that God knows our needs even before we ask Him, and we were in for a miracle.

One of my mother's classmates from Loma Linda Academy, Dr. Hertha Ehlers, was now head of the Department of Pediatrics for the College of Medical Evangelists, and she was also the head of the Pediatric Clinic for the White Memorial Hospital in Los Angeles.

After praying earnestly for the baby raccoons, who should arrive to visit us but Dr. Ehlers as an answer to our prayers. Erling took his baby raccoons to Dr. Ehlers right away. She immediately started giving him directions. "Erling, weigh each of the baby raccoons," she said. She studied their weight. She was obviously worried about them becoming dehydrated. It was clear that the baby raccoons condition was really serious. Dr. Ehlers wrote a prescription for a sulfa drug, and then she had my mother make rice water. If I remember correctly, the rice water and the sulfa drug were then put in the canned milk and stirred. Then the milk was put in the premature nursing bottle. The babies were so weak that we had to use the syringe to help them drink, or they would not live.

The baby raccoons started improving after just one feeding of Dr. Ehlers' formula. It truly was a miracle of modern medicine. Dr. Ehlers is such a wonderful woman because she cared for Erling's baby raccoons just as seriously as if they were people. She was respectful of Erling, a young boy with a strong desire to take good care of his pet raccoons.

In no time at all, the baby raccoons were well. Erling used to walk in front of the babies, and they would follow in single file. Our Grandpa Mac and Uncle Roland took pictures of them—both movies and slides. I think that Erling had a camera too, and he took pictures of the raccoons.

I believe *The Washington Post* asked if they could write a story on Erling's baby raccoons. Of course, Erling said yes. They took pictures of Erling holding a baby raccoon in one hand with all four little paws wrapped around the bottle, drinking. Plus they wrote a story about Erling and his adorable baby raccoons. I wish you could have seen them—they were so cute.

There were two males and two females. Erling was quite thoughtful and decided to sell one male and one female. But he kept one male and one female. The two he kept he named Punch and Judy. They were very healthy and beautiful besides being quite inquisitive. And you know, they seemed to have a sense of humor. They always went through Erling's trash can in his room to see if there was anything of interest.

Thanks to his raccoons, Erling was asked to give nature talks and teach others about God's amazing creation and the wonderful world of nature. His pet raccoons truly were a blessing to many children, young people, and adults.

Muriel

Chapter 6

The Spinning Song

My mother always tucked me in at night and had me say my prayers. One night a little while later, I heard my dad begin to play the Steinway grand piano in our living room. Dad was a fine pianist and a wonderful piano teacher. I loved listening to him play as I fell asleep. Dad's playing was so beautiful that it made me feel like I was very close to heaven.

I quickly realized that my mom had gone to her sister's or grandma's house, which was not far away, because Dad always practiced the piano when he was alone.

I quietly got out of bed and went to the hall where I sat down with my feet dangling through the banister. After sitting there quietly for a few minutes, I called, "Dad, please play the *Spinning Song.*" That song, which was composed by Mendelssohn, was my favorite piece that dad played.

Dad said, "Muriel, can't you tell that I am busy."

"Please, Dad, play the *Spinning Song*," I begged.

He gave in to my request and played my favorite piece. How I loved it! If I could persuade him to play the *Spinning Song* twice, I knew it was safe to come down the stairs and sit on the floor next to the keyboard where I would pull my flannel nightgown, which grandma had made me, over my toes to keep them warm while I listened to Dad play the piano or tell me stories about his childhood.

My daddy used to talk about how beautiful music like the Spinning Song inspires people.

But he would always remind me that the most beautiful music we have here on earth does not even compare to the beautiful music we will have when we get to heaven. Isn't that wonderful?

One day I told grandma about how much I loved the *Spinning Song*. Grandma then told me that she loved the *Spinning Song*, too and that her mother, my Great Grandma Eastman, loved it as well.

Grandma said, "You know, it sounds like the whirl of the spinning wheel as my mother spun the yarn when I was a little girl."

Not long ago I was talking to the neighbors I grew up with, Janet and Elaine. They told me that they always kept their window open, weather permitting, so they could listen to my dad play the piano while they were going to sleep.

To this day, when I hear the *Spinning Song*, it reminds me of the special times I spent with my dad listening to him play the piano.

Chapter 7

Dad's Bicycle

When my dad was a kid, he lived in Pasadena, California. He was fortunate to grow up around his grandparents from his mother's side. His grandfather, Grandpa West, was quite a character, but he was extremely genial. Great Grandpa West had fought in the Civil War when he was a teenager. He had been left for dead on the battlefield in Gettysburg, but he obviously wasn't dead or I wouldn't be here. Needless to say, he received gold medals from the United States of America for his bravery and service in the Civil War.

Now many years later, he was settled in Pasadena with a wife, children, and grandchildren. He owned a grocery store in the area, which people loved to come to and buy their groceries. Great Grandpa West ran such a fine business that one of the big chain grocery stores in the area decided to build a store across the street from Great Grandpa West and put him out of business by stealing his customers.

But it didn't seem to matter what the big grocery store did, they couldn't put Great Grandpa West out of business. His customers simply loved to talk with him. Plus, he gave his customers credit if they needed it. Wouldn't you know it, he put the big grocery store completely out of business!

Great Grandpa West did have a problem though. He had a terrible time asking his customers to pay their bills. This caused them to experience financial challenges from time to time.

Well, Great Grandpa West was not the only character in the family. His wife, Great Grandma West (who simply loved potatoes) was a real character too. One day Great Grandma West decided to take financial matters into her own hands, so she asked my dad, her grandson, if he would ride her around on his bicycle to collect the money from great grandpa's customers who had received credit from him. Mind you, Great Grandma West was wearing a long dress. (This was before women wore shortened dresses.)

When Dad would tell me this story, he would chuckle and chuckle at this point in the narration. He said, "Imagine how funny it must have looked with me, a kid, taking my grandmother on my bicycle, with her in a long dress, to collect money from grandpa's customers." At this point in the story, my dad's eyes would get all watery, and he would silently shake from laughing so hard.

My dad never talked about people much, so it was difficult to get him to tell you stories about his childhood. But I always enjoyed this one, which he told me more than once, about his grandparents.

Erling and Muriel

Chapter 8

The Good Deed

When I was growing up, Daddy had worship with us every morning, first thing, even when I was a preschooler. When I started elementary school, Daddy had worship with us before we went to school.

One day our Sabbath School lesson was about how God records our good deeds in heaven. Daddy looked at me and asked me if I knew what he was talking about. I shook my head and said, "No." I felt embarrassed because I didn't know the answer, and I worried about if I was doing what I should, because I really wanted to do everything just as Jesus wanted me to do.

Daddy kindly replied, "I didn't think you knew what I was talking about. When you do something good,

God records your deeds in a book in heaven."

Daddy continued, "On earth, I am your father, and I represent God who is your Father in heaven. I want you to love God in heaven, so I want to be the very best father on earth so that you will love your Father in heaven and do what He asks of you. You must obey Him."

A few days later, Daddy took me to Washington Missionary College, the Seventh-day Adventist college near our home. We entered a building that housed a recording studio. Daddy said, "I want to show you what a recording is."

So he sat down at the beautiful grand piano and started playing. What Daddy chose to play was exquisitely beautiful. It sounded heavenly to me, so I was very surprised when he stopped playing and acted quite upset. He had made a mistake. After talking to the man behind the glass in the recording booth, Daddy began again after the man gave him the signal. They repeated this process quite a few times. Finally, Daddy smiled and said that the recording was just perfect. The man in the recording booth finished his work and handed Daddy the record, and we took it home with us.

A week or two later, Daddy took Mother and me back to the recording studio at Washington Missionary College. After arriving at the studio, Daddy told me, "I want you to sing *I Found A Snowman*." I had just sung this song at a recital at the Washington Sanitarium and Hospital. I had practiced hard and knew it well. I nodded seriously and agreed to sing it for the recording.

Well, that was easier said than done. I sang and Mother accompanied me, but Daddy would stop us often to help me with my interpretation or correct my mistakes. Daddy stopped me quite a few times just like he had stopped and corrected himself. It was much more difficult to make a good recording than I had anticipated.

Finally, we did it one final time. Daddy then went behind the glass into the booth to listen to the recording Mother and I had made. He emerged with the finished record and said that it was perfect.

I was relieved that the process was done, but I felt quite proud that I was important enough to make a record.

It touched my little heart to think that my daddy would take the time and effort to teach me how wonderful our Father in heaven is to us. And you know, I never had any trouble loving our Father in heaven after that Sabbath School lesson and my father's loving actions toward his daughter.

Chapter 9

My First Baseball Bat

I was in fourth grade when this story took place. It was recess time, and our class was just learning how to play baseball. This was a new sport for me, but I was not very good at it, and this disturbed me quite a bit. After thinking things over very seriously, I decided to discuss it with my dad.

I got up my courage to approach Dad one evening after he had finished teaching his piano students for the day. This was not an easy subject for me to approach because I was very embarrassed that I needed help. And I really felt stupid that I could not play baseball better.

Finally, I told Dad I couldn't play baseball very well and everyone was playing baseball at school. Then I asked him if he could help me.

Dad was a wonderful listener who heard the whole story before offering suggestions. Needless to say, he quietly listened to my request before responding that, yes, he would be willing to help me learn how to play baseball.

A day or so later Dad suggested that he had time to help me play baseball. But before we began, he went to his woodworking shop in the basement. Emerging back upstairs, he entered the room with a bat and ball for us to practice with. To show you how important this was, Dad had made me a bat, just my size, to practice with. He had made it from scratch with his lathe. And he had even taken the time to stain it a rich brown. It had quite a bit of weight to it so that you could really hit the ball far.

I felt quite special to have my own bat, so we set off for the backyard. Dad demonstrated first, showing me how to swing the bat, and then it was my turn to swing the heavy bat. But soon I got the hang of it. Dad pitched the ball over and over to me so that I could practice batting. He was a good pitcher, and I was hitting the ball in no time.

Then Dad and I played catch. I can still remember how my fingers hurt as I was learning to catch the ball. Sometimes he threw the ball high so it would be like catching a pop fly. Finally, Dad asked me to pitch the ball and let him bat. He had me do this quite a while. All of this was excellent practice. Dad was a wonderful teacher, and I made quite a bit of progress.

Because of these private lessons, I really started to enjoy playing baseball. And I must have been successful in learning how to play the sport, because in fifth grade I was usually chosen for the position of permanent pitcher. That was an honor!

Chapter 10

The Guest

I was twelve years old and had just started attending a new school. I was in the process of making some new friends when I got an idea about the best way to accomplish this. So I approached Dad about my plan.

"Dad, would you play the piano for my new friend?"

Dad responded with a question. "What would you want me to play?'

I thought about what pieces I loved. There was, of course, the *Spinning Song* by Mendelssohn, but instead, I said, "There is a piece that I love where you cross your hands many times and it is all over the piano. I don't know the name of it, but it is simply beautiful. Could you play that?"

Dad said, "Oh, you mean this." And he played a few bars of Liszt's *Etude in D Flat*.

"Yes, that's the one," I said. "Can you also play *The Blue Danube Waltz* of Johann Strauss Jr.?"

What he was playing was *The Blue Danube* arranged by Schulz-Evler, which is a very delightful fun version. "Also, I want you to play the *Saint-Saen Swan Transcription* by Godowsky. But first, I want you to play the original of *Saint-Saen*, then play Godowsky's Transcription so that she can hear what Godowsky did."

Dad looked at me seriously and said, "I would need at least two weeks to practice before I would be ready to play for your friend."

Unbothered by the timeframe, I continued with my plan. "Dad, do you think Mom would let my friend come for dinner too?"

Dad said he did not know. He told me that I would have to ask Mom. He said he would be happy to play for my new friend but I must give him time to practice before he played.

With the entertainment portion of my plan in place, I proceeded to go and find Mom to talk about dinner. "Mom, could I invite my new friend over for dinner? I asked Dad if he would play for her, and he said yes, as long as I gave him time to practice."

Without waiting for a response, I continued, "Could we use our good china, and the goblets, and our good silverware?"

Mom slowed me down and asked, "What do you want to eat? I need your ideas for the menu." With Mom's approval, we began planning for my important get together.

I have forgotten what the exact menu was, but I do remember that we chose Scandinavian fruit soup for dessert. This is made with raspberries, pineapple, bananas, whipping cream, and tapioca. It is delicious to say the least!

After weeks of waiting, the day finally arrived when my new friend was coming to dinner. Mom and I had prepared as much of the food as we could the day before so that we could be sure that everything was done well.

I set the dining room table, putting the silverware on just like Mom had taught me to, straight with a napkin underneath the fork. I got all this done before my guest arrived. Mom even let me use the gold covered teak sherbet glasses for the Scandinavian fruit soup.

Dad put on a fabulous performance for my friend. I had her stand right beside the keyboard so she could watch his hands.

This special evening that I planned with my folks helped me to recognize and appreciate what a wonderful blessing I had taken for granted before. The love of my parents was beyond measure, just like the love of my heavenly Father.

We invite you to view the complete
selection of titles we publish at:

www.AspectBooks.com

Scan with your mobile
device to go directly
to our website.

Please write or email us your praises, reactions, or
thoughts about this or any other book we publish at:

ASPECT Books

www.ASPECTBooks.com

P.O. Box 954
Ringgold, GA 30736

info@AspectBooks.com

Aspect Books titles may be purchased in bulk for
educational, business, fund-raising, or sales promotional use.
For information, please e-mail:

BulkSales@AspectBooks.com

Finally, if you are interested in seeing
your own book in print, please contact us at

publishing@AspectBooks.com

We would be happy to review your manuscript for free.